This is the story of a road, and a battle. It is the story of Newton Road.

Newton Road is in an ___ ___ Sally ___ ___ ves there, near her school. She  all house, but she is happy. S ___ ___ ___ ces Newton Road. She li ___ ___ ___ ner neighbours like her. Newto ___

One day Sally is walking to her school. The school is in Newton Road too. She sees her neighbours, Helen Taylor and Paul Johnson. They are talking.

'Hello,' Sally says. 'What's happening?'

'Hello, Sally,' they say. 'Look! Look at this!'

Sally looks and sees this:

> **IMPORTANT**
> To the people of
> Newton Road
> Public Meeting
> Saturday March 1st
> 10.00 a.m.
> Please come to this public
> meeting. It is important.
> **Come to the Town Hall**
> THIS IS YOUR MEETING.
> COME!

Sally Robson thinks: 'I don't like this. Why is there a meeting in the Town Hall? Why is it important? People are happy here. We have no problems.'

'What's this about?' Helen Taylor says.

'I don't know,' Sally says. 'But I don't like it.'

She says goodbye to her neighbours and walks to school. She is thinking about Saturday, and the meeting.

Saturday comes, and the people of Newton Road go to the Town Hall. A man comes into the room.

'Good morning,' he says. 'My name is Wood. I'm a civil engineer.'

'A civil what?' Helen Taylor asks Sally.

'A civil engineer,' Sally says. 'Civil engineers build roads and houses.'

Mr Wood hears her. 'That's right,' he says. 'And I'm going to build houses for you. I'm going to build a new road too. But first I'm going to knock down the old houses in Newton Road. The new road is going to be there.'

'You're going to knock down our houses?' the people say.

'Yes,' Mr Wood says. 'But you live in old houses now. You're going to live in beautiful new houses.'

'Where are these beautiful new houses?' Sally asks. 'Are they near here?'

'No – no, they aren't,' Mr Wood says. 'But that's not important.'

'Yes, it is,' Sally says. 'We want to stay near our friends and our jobs. That's very important.'

Mr Wood is not happy. 'I'm sorry,' he says, 'but think about the new houses.'

But the people of Newton Road think about their friends and neighbours. 'What are we going to do?' they ask.

'We're going to stay in Newton Road,' Sally says. 'Mr Wood can't build a new road. Newton Road is our road. This is a battle – the battle of Newton Road.'

It is Monday. Sally Robson is at school. She tells her students about the meeting. She tells them about Mr Wood and the new road.

'He can't build a new road here,' they say. 'He can't knock down the houses and our school.'

But Mr Wood is a clever man. He shows the new houses to Helen Taylor. He shows them to Paul Johnson.

'Mr Wood isn't a bad man,' Helen Taylor tells Sally. 'And the new houses aren't bad.'

'They're very good,' Paul Johnson says. 'And they have big gardens. 'Think about that.'

Sally tells them: 'New houses and big gardens aren't important. Friends are important. And a school for your children.'

Stephen and Catherine are two of Sally Robson's students. They go to her house.

'The people want the new houses,' Sally Robson tells them. 'We can't win this battle.'

'Yes, we can, Miss Robson,' Stephen says. 'Our friends can help.'

Their friends come to Sally's house. Her neighbours see them. They say: 'Sally Robson is right. Friends are important. Newton Road is important.'

April comes. Sally Robson and her neighbours don't go to the new houses. They stay in Newton Road.

April goes and May comes. May goes and June comes. The people of Newton Road stay there.

'I can wait,' Mr Wood says.

June goes and July comes. July goes and August comes. Now Mr Wood isn't very happy.

'I can't wait,' he says. 'It's August. I'm going to build the new road. The people of Newton Road want a battle. They can have a battle!'

On Monday Mr Wood comes to Newton Road. His men are with him. The men have yellow machines. The machines are big. They can knock down houses.

'I'm going to build the new road,' Mr Wood says.

'No!' Sally Robson says. 'You can't come here with the machines. Look!'

The people of Newton Road are sitting in the road. Stephen and Catherine and their friends from school are sitting with them.

Mr Wood isn't happy. 'Wait,' he says to his men.

Mr Wood goes to the gas company. He talks to a man there. He goes to the electricity company and talks to a man there. He goes to the water company.

'Yes, I can help you,' the man at the water company says.

In the afternoon Mr Wood comes to Newton Road.

'You can stay here,' he says to the people. 'You can stay here, but you can't have gas in your houses. You can't have electricity, and you can't have water.' He looks at Sally. 'I'm sorry, but you want this battle. I don't. Battles aren't good.'

'What are we going to do?' the people ask.

Sally Robson thinks. 'Wait here,' she says. 'I'm going to telephone.'

She goes to a telephone. She talks to a newspaper man.

'Yes, my newspaper can help you,' the man says.

The man from the newspaper comes to Newton Road. He talks to Sally Robson. He talks to Helen Taylor and Paul Johnson. He talks to Stephen and Catherine and the children from the school.

'This is a good story,' he says. 'I can help you.'

The people of Newton Road say: 'We're winning this battle.'

It's Saturday morning. Stephen and Catherine show the newspaper to Sally Robson. She looks at it.

'THE BATTLE OF NEWTON ROAD,' the newspaper says. 'TEACHER AND STUDENTS IN BATTLE FOR HOMES. CAN THEY SAVE THEIR ROAD?'

'Our photographs are in the newspaper, Miss Robson,' Catherine says. 'Look. We're famous.'

And they *are* famous. The battle of Newton Road is famous. Helen Taylor and Paul Johnson have their photographs in the newspaper, too.

The people in the town talk about the battle. Some people say: 'Sally Robson and her friends are right. Friends and neighbours are important. Newton Road is their road.'

But some people say: 'Mr Wood is right. We want new roads in this town. The old roads are bad. New roads are very important. Build a new road. The people of Newton Road can go to the new houses.'

And some people say: 'Sally Robson is right, but Mr Wood is right too. What are they going to do?'

Now it is September. Mr Wood is thinking. He thinks of Sally Robson. 'Yes, she's right. Friends and neighbours *are* important.'

Sally is thinking too. She thinks: 'Mr Wood isn't a bad man. He's a civil engineer, and civil engineers build new roads. New roads are important. People want new roads.'

Stephen and Catherine are talking. 'It's a big battle,' Catherine says.

'And Miss Robson can't win it,' Stephen says. 'The people don't want a battle.'

'And it's September. We're going back to school.'

'What are we going to do?'

'I have an idea,' Catherine says. 'Come with me, Stephen. We're going to the Town Hall. We're going to talk to Mr Wood.'

Stephen and Catherine go to the Town Hall. Then they go to Newton Road. The people are happy there. 'We have gas in our houses,' they say. 'We have electricity and water. We're winning the battle.'

'What's happening? What's Mr Wood doing?' Sally Robson asks. 'We have gas and electricity. We have water. What's happening?'

'Mr Wood wants to visit Newton Road,' Stephen says.

'He wants a meeting,' Catherine says.

'A meeting for the people of Newton Road?'

'Yes, but not in the Town Hall. In Newton Road School.'

Stephen and Catherine go to the school. They see the headmaster, Mr Morgan.

'Yes, we can have a meeting here,' Mr Morgan says. 'We can have the meeting on Saturday.'

On Saturday the people of
Newton Road go to the school.
Mr Wood comes too.

'People of Newton Road,' he
says, 'you're right. You want your
friends and neighbours, and you can
have them. I don't want a battle.'

'Can we stay in Newton Road?'
Sally Robson thinks.

'You can have your friends and neighbours,' Mr Wood
says, 'but you can have your new houses too. We're going to
build new houses in a new road. The road has a new school
too. Mr Morgan can be the headmaster. You can stay with
your friends. It can be your road.'

'Our road?' the people say.

Mr Wood looks at Sally Robson.

'Robson Road!' he says.

13

'Robson Road! Yes, good idea!' the people say.

'No!' It's Sally Robson. 'No!' she says. 'It *isn't* a good idea. Robson Road isn't a good idea. We can stay with our friends in Newton Road. The new Newton Road.'

Mr Wood smiles. 'Yes,' he says. 'It can be the new Newton Road.'

The people of Newton Road smile. 'The new Newton Road,' they say. 'Good idea!'

Newton Road – the new Newton Road – is a happy road. Sally Robson lives there. Helen Taylor and Paul Johnson live there too. Mr Morgan is headmaster of the new school. The people are happy. They have new houses, but they have their old friends and neighbours.

Stephen and Catherine visit Sally Robson. Mr Wood visits Sally Robson too. He is her friend now.

'Your new house is good,' Mr Wood says.

'It isn't bad,' Sally Robson says.

'My new road is good,' Mr Wood says.

'Hmm!' Sally says.

Stephen and Catherine laugh. 'It's going to be a new battle,' Stephen says.

'A new battle of Newton Road,' Catherine says.

Sally Robson thinks. Then she laughs and says, 'No. Battles aren't good. Let's say "no" to battles!'

'"No" to battles!' Mr Wood says, and he laughs too.

ACTIVITIES

Pages 1–7

Before you read

1 Read the Word List at the back of the book. What are the twenty words in your language?

2 Look at the picture on pages 6–7. What do you think?

   a Who are the people in the picture?

   b What are they doing, and why?

While you read

3 Are these sentences right (✓) or wrong (✗)?

   a Sally Robson doesn't like public meetings.   .....

   b Mr Wood is going to build a new road.   .....

   c The people of Newton Road can stay in their houses.   .....

   d Sally doesn't want the new road.   .....

   e Her neighbours don't like the new houses.   .....

   f Friends are important in Newton Road.   .....

   g Mr Wood brings machines to Newton Road.   .....

   h The people of Newton Road watch from their houses.   .....

After you read

4 Work with a friend. Talk about the problem of Newton Road.

   a *Student A:* You are Mr Wood. The new road is important to the town. Tell Sally why.

       Student B: You are Sally. Your home is important to you. Tell Mr Wood why.

   b *Student A:* You are Sally. Why does Paul want to move? Ask questions.

       Student B: You are Paul Johnson. You want a big, new house. Answer Sally's questions.

Pages 8–15

Before you read

5 Why is Mr Wood talking to people at the gas, electricity and water companies? What is going to happen in Newton Road? Talk to a friend about these questions.

While you read

6 What happens first? And then? Write the numbers 1–8.

a People in the town start to talk about the road.   .....

b The houses in Newton Road have gas, electricity
and water again.   .....

c The newspaper man talks to her neighbours and
to students.   .....

d Sally talks to a man from a newspaper.   .....

e There is a public meeting at the school.   .....

f Stephen and Catherine talk to Mr Wood at the
town hall.   .....

g Sally and her neighbours move to a new Newton
Road.   .....

h He writes a story about the battle of Newton Road.   .....

After you read

7 Finish this sentence. Then show your sentence to your friends. Have they got the same answer?

..... win(s) the battle of Newton Road, because .....

8 What happens in the story? In which month? Write about the battle.

March: Public meeting about the new road

9 Write about your neighbours. Why are they (not) important to you?

WORD LIST *with example sentences*

battle (n) The *Battle* of Waterloo was in Belgium in 1815.

civil engineer (n) There is a problem with this new road. Who were the *civil engineers*?

company (n) The *company* makes cars and buses.

electricity (n) We can't watch television because there is no *electricity*.

gas (n) The house isn't near a town, and there is no water or *gas*.

happen (v) What *happened* to the people in the story?

headmaster (n) I like the *headmaster* and the teachers at my school.

help (v) Can you *help* me with my homework, please?

idea (n) I've got an *idea*! Let's go to London for the weekend.

knock down (v) A car *knocked* him *down*, but he is going to live.

laugh (v) She never stops *laughing*. She is a very happy child.

machine (n) That *machine* washes floors very well.

meeting (n) There is a *meeting* at school about the new buildings.

neighbour (n) My *neighbours* can see into my garden from their bedroom window.

public (adj) Of course the children can play here. These are *public* gardens.

save (v) That boy can't get out of the river. *Save* him!

show (v) Is that a new dress in your bag? *Show* me!

tell (v) They are going to *tell* us about their holiday in India.

town hall (n) We don't want new buildings here. Let's go and talk to people at the *town hall*.

win (v) I watch Manchester United because they *win* a lot of games.

Pearson Education Limited
Edinburgh Gate, Harlow,
Essex CM20 2JE, England
and Associated Companies throughout the world.

ISBN: 978-1-4058-7694-0

First published by Penguin Books 2000
This edition first published by Pearson Education 2008

3 5 7 9 10 8 6 4

Copyright © Pearson Education Ltd 2008
Illustrations by Alistair Adams

Typeset by Graphicraft Ltd, Hong Kong
Set in 12/14pt Bembo
Printed in China
SWTC/03

Published by Pearson Education Ltd in association with
Penguin Books Ltd, both companies being subsidiaries of Pearson Plc

For a complete list of the titles available in the Penguin Readers series please write to your local
Pearson Longman office or to: Penguin Readers Marketing Department, Pearson Education,
Edinburgh Gate, Harlow, Essex CM20 2JE, England.